post parting

Nida Rashid

BookLeaf
Publishing

India | USA | UK

Made with ❤ on the BookLeaf Publishing Platform
www.bookleafpub.in
www.bookleafpub.com

Dedication

to my first born, who made me a mother

Acknowledgements

Ali, the best partner and father, it takes two

My incredible birth support team: Fariba, Corrine, Kayla and Zainab.

Thank you, Nadira Baig, for your insightful comments and encouragement in the poetic process.

Preface

Post parting contains a collection of poems and thoughts that came from the depths of postpartum as I processed the intensity of labour for the first time. Post parting is what comes after the parting of mother and child from the womb into the world.

Amidst the sleepless nights and physical exhaustion, I was not able to form many coherent thoughts. With a newborn to take care of, the mind goes into a lull that focuses only on the survival of this little human. While poetry typically helps process and explore life's most difficult moments, the thought of poems was far from my mind until a single moment struck me.

Two months after I had given birth, a visitor casually stated: 'A child is like a parasite – it takes everything from you'.

I don't know why those words shocked me, but they initiated an overflow of thoughts as I tried to process the truth of how I felt.

Hadn't I been struggling with sleepless nights, felt like my life is no longer my own? Hadn't I been depleted, completely taken over? I should have vehemently agreed with the statement, even if it was a joke. But for some reason, it made me deeply uncomfortable, and I stayed up all night – this time not to soothe my baby but to think about what it means to have a baby.

Even though this statement was not new to me, it caught me off guard only this time. The last time I heard this was in the first trimester of my pregnancy, in the doctor's office. I had expressed concern that I wasn't eating enough to sustain my baby, and the doctor casually said,

'Your baby is like a parasite; it will take what it needs'.

At that time, that analogy was comforting. But 9 months later, after all the exhaustion, hearing that analogy again struck me. Because now this baby was a reality, no longer a blood clot. And while this baby was still sucking out my reserves of energy, I could not understand the analogy of parasite anymore.

That was the moment I began to write again, poem after poem, every day for twenty-one days. These twenty-one poems are in no particular order but were a part of an effort to process the novelty of motherhood.

Doctor Mom

The White-Coated doctor smiled as she
listened to my list of symptoms.
Congratulations, you have a cute little
parasite.

White Coat:

A parasite, a persistent thief.
It drinks the blood; it steals the air,
Unseen, it grows without a care.

The Rising Mother in me replied:

It's like a parasite? What a relief!
Yes, my little fetus, take what you need
Survive while I suffer; grow strong, I plead

White Coat:

This parasite will take from you to thrive
As it clings, it holds, it stays,
In fragile forms, in every phase

The Rising Mother in me replied:

Yes, I want it so desperately to survive
I thank God
As I hear the gallop of its heartbeat
And feel the kick of its tiny feet

White Coat:

It continues to weaken you, the host
So in the darkness, a truth is clear:
There'll be pain, and danger to fear

Mother:

You've reduced me to a body, at most
But you cannot take away how I feel
The fact is, in my love for it, I heal

My Blood

The cycle of monthly mourning
Paused to transform into your nest
It's as if each time you weren't there
I shed blood in despair

Finally, I can grow and become your home
I have made space and grown
I have shifted aside solid structures, so
well-known
and routine systems now accommodate my
new goal

You were just a blood clot, nested inside my
blood
But isn't it interesting that our blood is not
shared?
A different type of blood runs through your
veins
By all other definitions, you should have been
foreign

Don't Cry Over...

On your father's cotton blue t-shirt is a large
white stain,
but he wears it like a badge of honour in your
name.
Spit milk.
On our brand-new beige sofa, there's a wet
spot settling in,
we can still see the traces of white residue on
your chin.
Spit milk.
On the dressing table by the door, there's a
heap of wet clothes,
Day by day, our pile of laundry grows.
Spit milk.
On the green blanket, we laid down on the
floor,
there's a thick puddle left to adore.
Spit milk.

each one reveals
that you're satisfied
and full after your meals
as you grow,

you are marking this territory
as your home
and with each stain,   5
you claim us as your own

Wonder

When your beautiful, big eyes glance up at
the sky
I hope you wonder how it's held so high
When you see the sunset at the end of each
day
I hope you wonder why it goes away
When you see the phases of the moon shining
bright
I hope you wonder where it gets its radiant
light
When you see the stars that darkness cannot
hide
I hope you wonder who they are set to guide
When your beautiful eyes slowly come to rest
I hope you wonder what wonders you'll see
next

Opening Ceremony

They cut the ribbon between us
And left us both wounded
I had a giant hole in my body
In the space you left
You had a stump on your belly
And cried in distress

You are now open to the world!

It brings growth and adventure
beautiful knowledge to gain
But it brings struggle and trials
as you are now open to its pain

But the world is now open to you, too
Your character, your smile, your care
your heart, your mind, your prayer

They cut the ribbon and split us into two
now, between us is the entire world's view
slowly we'll heal,
and I'll watch you become
you.

Shock

A drastic transition
You have come from darkness into light
And you protest with your eyes shut tight
I have come from the brink of death
Transformed into a mother with your breath

Unraveled

Your tiny little hands have reached out and
untangled a thread from inside me

I see the thread grow longer with your tug
the tangled fabric I have spent years weaving
is coming undone,
you are revealing parts of me
I don't quite understand
you are tugging on memories I'd forgotten I
had
I will pick up the threads you've picked out
And weave myself into someone new

Expand

Can someone please explain to me how the
heart expands?
How does it work when I feel a pang?
Does the muscle grow and bulge from
increased demand?
Or does it borrow supply from a nearby
gland?

Does it remove an artery to keep blood from
escaping?
And exactly what happens when the heart is
aching?
How can I be whole when I feel it's breaking?
Do the chambers divide into more than just
four?
Or do veins get added for blood to pour?

However it happens, however it goes
Please tell me, whoever knows
Because what my heart feels for this child of
mine
feels beyond reason, feels divine.

Coffee Shop Stories

A woman with a blue pashmina around her
neck
is sipping her coffee by the window
she sits alone at a table for four
a young man with headphones
sits in the corner
scrolling through his phone, he is
completely unaware as we walk through the
door.

I catch pieces of conversation here and there:

'What is wrong with youth these days?'
'...and just like that, she threw her phone!'
'I'll go to Costco to get beef tenderloin trays.'
'After twenty-nine years, she left me alone.'

But as I stroll through the shop trying to find
a chair,
an older lady immediately turns, 'Baby'! she
squeals
she slowly peers over your cover and sees
Another old man smiles with delight

'Oh, I remember those days.'
Another man chimes in,
'How much sleep are you getting at night?'

It was as if you hit pause
on all the stories in the coffee shop
as everyone turned around to look
at the new story that just begun

Cycle of Life

Your wide eyes
hold deep sighs
yet they follow me
with unwavering loyalty
As you look to me for care
and trust me
completely unaware

Did every human start off this much in need?
For every adult standing,
there was someone
to hold, someone to feed
in the early days of vulnerability
I become aware of human fragility

Steer

I sat thinking about how I will steer the ship
of your life
navigate you through every storm
Guide you in the night by pointing to the
stars
always lead you back home

then I remember that I myself
do not wheel
I have been overcome by waves
and found multiple shores
I have sat staring out at the seas
sometimes standing tall
sometimes bent on my knees

but I was guided through
and so will you, my dear
because I completely trust the One
in whose Hands our stories steer

Baby, Baby, Me

Feed, burp, complete
Change, sleep, repeat
Wash, dry, back pain
Play, clean, complain
Spit, spill, provide
Reach, grab, wide-eyed
Ooh, Ahh, decode
Pee, poo, explode!
Cry, sing, assure
Hug, hold, secure

Standing Over

I stood
over a protruding mound
of flesh
bowed my head down
And whispered to you
through skin, flesh and blood
Through layers of darkness
I closed my eyes
and prayed

Life.

You may stand
over a protruding mound of fresh
dirt
bow your head down
and whisper to me
through grass, dirt and cloth
Through layers of darkness
You close your eyes
and pray

Flight

As soon as I received you at Arrivals
the call came for my gate at Departures
so the time we have together,
is the time spent in the airport

between customs and rites of passage
between crowds and carrying baggage
we might get lost in our own worries
routines and rituals might keep us occupied
through the many gates of life
and random checks that throw us back
as we head in opposite directions
let's not forget to sit still in the now
even if it is in the waiting area of an airport

Peace

our first meeting was rehearsed in my mind
multiple times,
eyes welled with tears, indescribable joy
And I'd welcome you into the world with the
words of peace
Just like the words used for Mary's son:
'Peace be upon me the day I was born'!*

when we were pulled apart
In the moments that made us two,
I was exhausted and numbed
'Salaam' was all I managed to whisper to you

I knew this was new
My days were in a daze
I was getting weaker by the week
And still, 'Salaam' was all I managed to speak

And now, as we grow stronger
My heart grows fonder
we begin every day
With the same words, as I say:
'Asalaamu Alaykum'**

*Quran: Chapter 19, Verse 33
**Peace be upon you.

S'mothered

no matter how many times I am asked
I can find no words to answer
'how does it feel to be a mother'
I sense anticipation as they wait
for something profound
a response to inspire awe
or create a reply of 'aww'
my mind draws blank
some mothers may say it feels wonderful
some others may say it feels overwhelming
smothered in daily tasks and worry

a title was ordained
but it's been but two days since I've reigned
ask me again when the one I claim
calls me by this new name

Blessed Worry

when you gasped for air
worry, like I never knew before
When you had an itch
worry, something deep in my core
the worry of your well-being
the worry of where you are
are you safe
are you warm
what's the norm?
worry was love in the newest form

but each worry that had me stressed
made me thankful to be blessed

when you finally took a breath
grateful, for every particle of air
when you finally felt relief
grateful, in every prayer
All praise is to the Lord
whose blessings continue to pour

Home

I want to be the one
you can always return to
the comfort and warmth you seek
whenever you need
the voice of unconditional love and
acceptance
when you try to find where you belong
the ears that will listen to your every
complaint
the heart that will feel your lows and your
highs
so here I am
starting now
cooing and gurgling back at you
responding to all your calls and cries
holding you close in the darkest night
arms wrapped around your tiny form
here we are, making a home

Wahn Ala Wahn

Weakness upon Weakness*
It's true
Hardship upon Hardship
It's new
Worry upon Worry
It's blue
Miracle upon Miracle
It's you.

*Quran: Chapter 31, Verse 14

Painting

Imagine I'm painting with all the colours life
has given me
My canvas is on an easel, dripping wet paint
and it falls onto
your blank canvas
take my colours
and use your tiny fingers
spread them around
To make your own canvas bright

Paradise

'Do you have a mother'?
'Stay with her, for Paradise is beneath her
feet'.*

I try to create a paradise for you.
make everything perfect
the best food at a single call
entertainment, comfort, play
you can have it all
at my own expense
but I'm human so
it's no paradise,
no matter how hard I try

To become a mother
Is to want paradise more for another

*Saying of the Prophet Muhammad, Peace be
Upon Him